The Rural Lives of Nice Girls

The Rural Lives

———of———

Nice Girls

Poems New and Selected

Gailmarie Pahmeier

Rainshadow Editions
The Black Rock Press
University of Nevada, Reno
2014

ISBN 978-1-891033-68-1
Library of Congress Control Number: 2014937551

Printed in the United States of America
First Printing: April 2014
Second Printing: January 2015
Third Printing: October 2018

The Black Rock Press
University of Nevada, Reno
Reno, NV 89557-0224

The publication of this book was supported by a
generous grant from the Nell J. Redfield Foundation

For Donald Jude, my very own saint, and dedicated to the memory of the real James Otis Brownlow Lawson and the very, very real Brenda Kay Pahmeier (too soon, sweet sister, too soon). Thanks to all of you for your stories, for your grace and faith.

Contents

Acknowledgements

The author gratefully acknowledges the following publications in which some of these poems originally appeared, some in earlier versions: *Pinyon Poetry, neon, Mudfish, Rio Grande Review, Weber Studies, Pedestal Magazine, Kokanee Review, Clover: A Literary Rag, Paddlefish, descant, Spillway, Booth, Passager, Gris-Gris,* and the *Berkeley Poetry Review.*

"Saving Face" originally appeared in *New Poets of the American West*, for which it received the Editor's Choice Award.

"I Miss Everyone in Amarillo" was commissioned for a traveling art exhibit, Always Lost: A Meditation on War.

"Story Problems" and a companion essay, "Love You Big: from Patsy Cline to Poetry" were commissioned for the anthology *Follow the Thread.*

Many of the poems in Part One appeared in a limited edition chapbook, *Shake It and It Snows*, which won the 2009 Coal Hill Chapbook Award from Autumn House Press.

Many of the poems in Part Two appeared in the limited edition chapbook, *With Respect for Distance*, published by Black Rock Press.

The author would also like to thank Sierra Arts Foundation for an artist's grant which made the making of some of these poems possible, and the Vermont Studio Center, Western States Arts Federation, and the Witter Bynner Foundation for a fellowship and residency during which some of these poems were originally conceived.

And finally, an abundance of gratitude goes to David Lee and Bob Blesse, those whose unwavering belief in the power of poetry is the most blessed thing; to everyone at the Nevada Arts Council for their professionalism, friendship, and financial support; to the arts community in Fallon, Nevada, especially Kirk Robertson and Valerie Serpa (best audiences in the world!); and to all the creative writing students at the University of Nevada, who inspire and challenge all of us lucky enough to work with them.

West of Snowball

When Shorlene's husband took up dying,
did it tear a hole the size of a cat's yawn
into the center of her heart?
Her man, Brownlow Otis Lawson,
was my godfather, a boy of twenty,
and dying the year I was born.
A mysterious lung disease devouring
him, the doctor told him to move
to Arizona, he couldn't breathe
in Arkansas or Missouri
he had to move to dry air. That part
of the story is true. My mother told
me Brownlow took up and off with Shorlene
two days after meeting her as she served
peach cobbler at the Bobber Cafe
in Snowball, Arkansas, right alongside
the Buffalo River in the land of angry
chiggers and an accent that smooths a *t*
to a *d*. First time Brownlow had a good
talk with her, Shorlene told him her simple
dream, that one day she'd own herself a few
banded holsteins, big beautiful white cows
with black rings about their thick bellies.
Brownlow heard her say *bandit* holsteins
and he imagined a life with this woman
who desired cows wearing Lone Ranger
masks, he imagined holding her, buying
her gin drinks, touching the chapped skin
of her hands. That night he drove her home
and away forever from the Bobber Cafe,
its rod and tackle decor, red and white
plastic bobbers, the kind children use
to fish a back pond on a grandmother's

1

farm, these trinkets dangling from each table
lamp. Brownlow drove Shorlene into the next
county to marry, she dozing against
his shoulder as the car jutted along
the back washboards. She awakened to the sound

of crunched bone, the boy's "shit" said softly
and under his breath. He'd run a rabbit down
and it was then she knew she could love him,
this sickly, imperfect boy who couldn't protect
anything, but he could let her sleep,
would always have a gentle whisper
in the dark. This was the year I was born.

Nearly thirty years later, the year I married
the man who made good on his promise
to take me West, my mother gave me
two beaten shoe boxes filled with letters
Brownlow had written to me in the last months
of his life. I came to know this boy who loved
me decades after his death. He wrote me,
a baby, letters, stories he had to give,
all that he had to give. This was the story
of a blue, but ordinary life.

If he'd lived to watch me come up,
would he have given me more, would I
have told him some stories? She who tells
the tale gets to name the monster, gets
the princess her perfect kiss, the children
all own shoes. Brownlow, if you'd lived
and if I'd loved you, these are some
of the stories I might have told you.

PART ONE

The writer needs an address, very badly needs
an address—that is his roots.
—Isacc Bashevis Singer

If you do all your growing up in the same small place,
you don't shed identities. You accumulate them.
—Tracy Kidder

Homegrown Roses

Everyone has a story to tell
that's set inside a bar. I remember
the long year I loved a boy from school,
how every day at five o'clock we met
at George's Lounge, how we became familiar,
the aging lady bartender calling
out in her clear voice—*Miller, Miller Lite*—
before that big door eased shut behind us.
I also recall being conscious
of the clock, how in the world of the tavern
you are always alive in the future,
even if it's only ten or fifteen
minutes, long enough to know the baseball
game you're watching is behind you, that if
you hope hard enough your team can still score,
there's time and plenty of it. Imagine,
too, one chilled summer night when I was young
and fleeing my first divorce, found myself
at the End of the Trail in Dayton, Nevada.
I met a man who bought me drinks, who fed
the jukebox till I thought it would burst,
held me close enough to hear his heart.
I don't remember when we decided
to pretend—this is a bar story,
after all—but we told the other patrons,
four tired cowboys and a black-eyed woman,
that we'd just been married, this was our
honeymoon and we were happy.
One of the cowboys wandered outside,
broke a rose from a battered bush, placed it
in a beer bottle, a gift for the bride.
I still have it. And now every year or so,
when I return to my truck in the dark

after work, I find a single rose anchored
under the wiper. My friends think I should
be afraid of this, as if this flower
were a dead chicken or a stalker's signature.
But it's just a rose and all it means
is that I'm forever joined to a man
who'll never know my real name, a man
I couldn't possibly pick out in a crowd.
Now, your turn. Tell me one of your stories.

Home Cooking

What I'm about to tell you is true.
It was in the paper some few years back,
but I'd forgotten until you asked
about my sister, asked if I thought
she was a pretty baby, asked if I'd
taken good care of her. The answers are *yes*.
She's the one with the rich red hair, my father's
clear grey eyes that can be blue, can be
startled into green. But that's not the story
I wanted to tell you. Here's what happened:

Somewhere in Florida a young woman worked
the counter at Bubba's Bodacious Bar-B-Q,
worked hard because she had a pretty
baby, a daughter she hoped would one day
ease into beautiful. People said, *that sure
is a pretty baby*, and she believed
them, too much a mother to own that that's
just what polite people say. She heard
talk about a children's beauty pageant
coming to town, and this could be her child's
ticket, but entry was fifty bucks
and how's she to get that when all she did
was wrangle ribs apart for customers
who never heard of ten percent. Now Bubba's
doing good, she figured, kept an extra
cash box. So late one night after all were gone,
she carried the big knife, the one Bubba
sharpened while he chewed and spit,
she carried this knife into the back dark
and jimmied open that box for fifty bucks.

I'll bet all that money shined with promise,
with the pure beauty of opportunity.
She can't remember hearing Bubba's footsteps,
how he came up behind her, how she turned,
and the knife, the big knife, sunk right into him.
What she'll always remember is how she
stood there in his blood and clutched twenty
dollar bills into nests, how she knew then
her daughter would never be beautiful,
would always hunger for the wrong things:
a boy to bring her a bag of blueberries,
his long, hard kiss, her heart wrapped in his hand.

Does this answer your questions? *Yes*, my
sister is both lovely and dangerous,
and *yes*, *yes*, we did the best we could.

Home Schooling

In the snapshot she loves, her grandmother
pours coffee into mismatched cups,
the biscuit cobbler still inside on the stove.
She's the two-year-old on Harriet's lap,
her other aunts (there's Thelma, there's Mabel,
there's pretty Jean) sit smoking and squinting
into the sun, their full, strong arms sleeveless
and shining, bare legs dangling off the porch.
Their men are somewhere with whiskey and dogs
(there'd be Gus, there'd be Otis, Arthur and Ike),
somewhere they are smoking their own cigarettes,
shooting cans off the fence line, swearing out loud.
She loves this snapshot because in it
everyone is still alive, still drinking ,
still full of voice and muscle and blood.
These women in the snapshot and their absent
men would reward her often for small things—
snagging a catfish before it swallowed
the hook, filling a jar with fireflies
to set out at the pump, bringing in
the first tomatoes. The prize was almost
always a sip of beer or a cup of coffee,
the promise of pie and salt to come.

In this snapshot she loves, her grandmother
pours coffee into mismatched cups,
waits for the soldiers or the sheriff
to the door, has long known to say, *come, sit,
let me get y'all something to drink, something
real good and real strong.*

Hometown Girl at 30

Someone more romantic might say
it has to do with the rhythm of spoons,
the toy piano sound of silverware
tossed onto a table. Someone else might
say it has to do with the way I move
across the floor, my thick-hosed legs aching
to be quick. All I can say is I like

waiting tables where truckers gulp my strong
coffee, tell lies they hope will loosen
my grip, lure me into their cabs come dark.
Sometimes I'm sorely tempted, and I've gone
to a few who were young and good-looking
and on their way to somewhere I might get
a card from. I like the big button

I wear pinned to my chest—*Try Our Famous
Cherry Cheesecake*—I like the way I make
things shine (napkin dispensers, the easy
necks of catsup bottles, the long counter
I rest my body against). I like the noise
of Alvie in the kitchen singing
"Delta Dawn," the sweet smell of onions

Roberta chops for chili, I love knowing
I'm at home here, another small town girl
with big dreams. I love knowing that someday
I will walk out of here on the arm
of someone with promise, that everyone
will miss me, will say, *Whatever happened
to that local gal who told those stories?*

Walking Away from Home

Nobody knows where the boxes came from,
only that they were always there, under
the sink, stacked high in a corner
of the closet—shoe boxes, shoe boxes
everywhere. My mother wrapped her gifts
in these—candies, hair ribbons, small sweaters ...
All I remember her giving me came
in an old Stride Rite or Hush Puppy,
the label blacked out with thick marker,
her own handwriting scrawled across the lid—
NOT SHOES. NOT SHOES. NOT SHOES.

My sister says the memory makes her
smile, helps her sort through our mother's things.
My sister asks again: What do you want?
I tell her all I want are those rhinestone
pumps our mother wore in her pageant days.
My sister finds this strange, and sad.
She doesn't understand that this time
all I want is a pair of shoes, I want
something beautiful but predictable,
I need to know exactly what I'm getting.

From this House to Home

Has he called in the cats now, made certain
all are accounted for, that their bellies
are full, that they have not become food
for coyotes come down into porch light
for water? Is he reading a book
under the cool warmth of our down
comforter, clearing his throat between
chapters as if he'd actually
uttered the words, lived in their world?
What is he doing right now? I am
feigning sleep in an iron bed in my hometown,
listening to the hum of air conditioner
and my parents' deep breathing. Today
we had our reunion in weather
so thick I could barely breathe. My clothes
were all wrong—the blue jeans and boots,
sweat streaming from under my cowboy hat—
brought sympathetic smiles from those in shorts
and cropped tees, their over browned bodies
glistening in games of horseshoes
and washers. The women chased children,
sought shade, stretched on blankets, shared
photographs. My sister brought potato
salad for fifty, cored onions
all afternoon, slipped fat slices of butter
and beef bouillon inside them, wrapped them
in foil for the grill, the smell of bratwurst
and beer a reminder of why we were there.
It was a good day, slow and full. But now
I am ready to return, to truly
come home, to him, to our house in the high
desert, our often angry way of life.
I don't belong here among women

wearing sundresses and sandals, clothes
the colors of Easter eggs. I'm coming
home, sooner than we'd planned. This is not
a place where women wear hats, and my family
is older now than I will ever know them.

Our Saturday Drive Toward Home

I eat powdered donuts from the box,
the sugar dusting my denim shirt.
He drives, sips coffee, fiddles with the radio.
Anyone who sees us at a stop sign
will think we're comfortable, two middle-aged
people out early. No one will know how
unsettled we feel, how eager we are
to fill our life with things. We're going to
garage sales, we're going antiquing.
I'm here this morning as his new lover,
and we're out to make a home together,
to furnish ourselves with a history
we have no time to create. There's an urgency
to our years, to our sense of common dream.

We'll load his truck all morning with our finds—
a hand-cranked ice crusher, a 1950's
highchair, a chaise lounge that'll cost a fortune
to reupholster. What we avoid
are the sad boxes of family photos
everyone seems willing to sell (that one
could be my German grandmother, prim
in her high collar, and that one could be
his great-uncle come down to town
from the Tennessee hills). We're honest enough
to know we need each other, know that we're
desperate for completion, but there's a boundary
to how far we'll go, how much of a bargain
to bargain for. So on this Saturday
we'll shop around, knowing at every stop
that this is surely that moment between
history and desire, that moment
which can only be filled with the feel

and smell of the familiar, and even
if it's earned in this dishonest way,
there's no turning back.

Calling Home

The man I love calls me *doll*, calls me *baby*.
He phones me everyday, *his sweet, sweet girl*.
Sometimes we talk about his mother,
how she lost thousands on worthless coins
she'd read about in the back of a magazine,
how it makes him sad to think of her alone,
wrapping the coins in doilies, trying
to save something as legacy.
I tell him about my grandmother,
her farm sold, her move to town, how she ate
cat food for months, how the clerks allowed
her to buy the cans, knowing she had
no barn, nothing left to feed. I tell him
that this made my father cry. He says he'll
never let anyone hurt me, that when I'm old
I'll still be his *sweet baby*, his
little doll. I try to imagine
an old man betrayed by circumstance,
by loneliness, but I can't. It's almost
always the women left behind to live.
Oh, Sweetie. My poor little baby doll.

Coming Home for the Cat

I know what she's going through. I know how
anyone who's loved a cat, allowed one
to sleep against her face, allowed one
to lay its full body along her outstretched
legs until they go numb, can grieve for months.
I once met a woman so attached
to her cat she couldn't imagine her
house without it, left the cat's body
on the coffee table, an honest wake,
until her grown son had had enough.
I know another who keeps her cat's ashes
on the mantle in a little cedar
box, *In Loving Memory* burned into
the lid, the cat dead some several years.
I even understand how hard it is
to get them to the vet. Cats, unlike dogs,
cannot be tricked into your truck.

And I understand because I used
to love a man who hurt me with his heart.
We had a cat. Sometimes I think if I
had not stopped loving him, if I had not
left for the arms of a boy who held me
as if I could break, that cat would be alive.
I would've been there to see the sores,
the open-mouthed breathing, I would've been
there to save her. That man saw nothing,
did little but bury her when she finally
gave in. At least that's something. I live
in another city now, too far away
to visit, but I'm sure she's an angel.
Yes, love for an animal can make you whole,
especially if it's all you've got for now.

Letter Sent Home: Please Hand Cancel

You know what I'm talking about, you've seen
the headlines too—how So and So Collapses
in an airport, a doctor diagnoses
exhaustion—how So and So goes away
to rest, to reclaim some sense of self. I always
imagined this luxury of tiredness
affordable only to the rich, movie stars
and rock 'n' roll celebrities, people
whose daily lives played out as documentary.
But now I know that's a lie, because
here I am on a spring morning so tired
I can taste a dream on my tongue. I've gone
away, left you to yard work, home maintenance,
the late afternoon walk to gather our mail.
I said I needed rest, a place to refuel.
I lied. I need much more than sleep, much more
than careless dreaming. Sometimes I lie so
much the truth's hard to tell and has a false
ring to it. Last night I dreamt we were making
love in an old hotel off Union Square, San Francisco.
We thrashed and clawed each other against
the rumble of delivery trucks below
our window, the sounds of a city
very much alive. Only after
we'd made our slow journey back into this
world did I look out the window, saw
the billboard—Ken Griffey, Jr., large as sky.
I knew then the dream was a lie, that I was
in the wrong city, with the wrong man, perhaps
even a bit player in someone else's
small blue dream. This is what some people call
a moment of truth, that tiny second
of clarity we liars hope to own but

only lease—no matter how earnestly,
no matter how often we pray. The truth,
in its raw, pure power truly's a gift
to be cradled. So there you have it.

I'll write again, I promise you that much.

Before You Leave Home, Remember This

I know you've come from some other woman.
The New Orleans night is all over your clothes.
You've watched me come out of mine
with the calculation you give things
earned and now owned.
See these thick breasts once
a high and proud prize in Georgia.
See these blue laced legs known early
as the smooth refuge of an eager heart.
See everything—see this band
embedded in the fullness of my finger,
bought those days we laughed at the lack of things:
Rent money, good meat, movies.
Remember that was in Florida
where every day came on white and clean.
And remember that I was a blonde.

A Home Full of Color

"Y'all have no idea how much it costs to look this cheap."
—Dolly Parton

I, too, believe in makeup, believe in
the luxurious artifice of color
that couldn't possibly come from within.
I want my eyelashes as long as spiders' legs,
my cheeks the startled tones of too much—
sun, drink, fevered loving—and my mouth
a darker, more defined wound. I love

most the men who aren't afraid, who'll kiss
my red lips straight on, take the color
onto their own, leave it there until
some other woman touches a tissue
to her tongue, rubs out my being there.
It is, indeed, expensive to be cheap.

Think of Jezebel, alone at her dressing
table, her meticulously rendered
applications—hands, hair, face, feet. She knows
they are coming to kill her, that her blood
will bracelet the hooves of horses,
perhaps even imagines her hands and feet
gnawed from their limbs but still lovely,

lovingly tendered, an offering of sorts.
I've lived long enough to know what can happen
to a face, to the body earned and deserved.
Applying makeup is a way of saying,
here's who I am, enhanced and ready for
anything. Come on now, come on and kiss me.

PART TWO

... he loved his daughter better even than his pipe, and
like a reasonable man and an excellent father, let her have
her way in everything.
—Washington Irving

If you had no family, you'd have no poems.
—Robert Pahmeier

Fathers With Daughters

Watching this one now in her painless sleep,
you imagine your eyes, her mother's limbs,
an odd mesh of familiarity.
A director with only an actor,
no script, you've a definite job to do.
Be precise, be consistent. Hold her head
In your lap in the late afternoons,
tell her she's lovely as soon as you're sure
she understands somehow what that might mean.
Your daughters are a perilous treasure,
an uncertain pleasure, a certain wish,
a work to be criminally proud of.
For men without sons there is always this.

The Swing

The yellow metal seat flashes
in the casual summer sun.
His four daughters, all under twelve
and desperate to be pushed
circle around him
as he waters the garden.

Swing me, Daddy!   *Swing me!*

You'd shoot the hose at us.
The water was hard and cold—right for August—
but then the sudden tilt to your laughter.
The neighbor paused to watch your girls
running, bare feet springing the dandelions,
skin sparkling and dripping.

When I pass the park at night now,
I imagine a father swinging his daughter,
pushing her higher, higher.
The park echoes long trailing screams of pleasure
as thick familiar hands propel her small body,
her skirt opening to gather the dark.

With Respect for Distance

Before I pull into the parking lot,
I see him standing there, shirt-sleeved, pipe in hand.
Since last week he hasn't changed,
perhaps he looks a little tired.
His slow smile and I know I'm on time.

How's she runnin'?
The certain first question, his greeting.
I give the shrug, tap the hood of my car.
There is something miraculous about this machine,
how it has come to cement a father and daughter
separated by everything but this link.

We pass the day calling trucks—
Peterbilt, Kenworth, Mack.
Small words, none as striking
as the glint of chrome beneath his determined touch.
When I leave, I know he is watching me,
waiting for the sound of malfunction.

What will I tell my children when he is gone?
He was a quiet man who could make things run.

My Mother's Story About the Dog

My father, one morning as always,
went to lift the aged terrier from her bed,
carried her to the kitchen, out the door.
He sat her in twenty-two inches of hard snow,
made coffee, wandered to the window.
He watched her circle the yard, turn toward him.
He thought she saw a bird or simply desired
to climb into the box under the porch
where she curled against herself in warmer weather.
But she quivered, she collapsed,
dragged herself mere inches through snow.

Days later my mother found my father
missing. His coat gone, she feared he'd left
toward the store, and with so many decent men
dying doing simple chores in the cold,
she called his name into the white with heart.
She found him safely bundled, breathing hard
to smooth into a slick mound the snow
above where the dog lay. He rose before her
brought a handful of snow to her mouth.
She ate from his palm, gathered snow to feed him.
This, she says, is what comes of it, of love.

Home Maintenance

Sometimes my father's hand shakes, sends fat drops
of paint to splatter my patio.
He's fond of this work, and I like the way
this man feels in the sun, healthy and honest
and responsible. I work next to him
on the shorter ladder, my hair sticky
against my neck. He says, *This heat's a bitch*.
I say, *Wears my ass out*. I'd like more talk,
but it's too hot, too hot to wrap our mouths
around vowels, urge consonants into
the air. We'll finish my house by Saturday,
my father will go home, live through another
familiar summer in his own backyard.
We both know he'll never be back, that this
job is his last large gift, that he will tell
my mother about the heat, tell her
this paint will last seven years at most,
that he worries about who will help me
next time, who will work beside me in the sun,
who will love me in ways simple as sweat.

Driving Dad to The Dog Museum

On cross country road trips, my father sang,
old songs he made us learn at least to hum,
my mother snapping along in the front seat,
their daughters untethered in the back.
He sang Oh, Susanna, he sang There's a Hole
In the Bucket, *dear Liza, dear Liza,*
he sang Maybellene (*why can't you be true?*),
songs with pet names for all of us.
Today I've sprung him from Assisted Living,
a picnic in the park, then the Dog Museum.
I'll pay to see the Huneck exhibit,
the wood cuts and chairs, admire
the exquisite porcelain Great Dane,
a harlequin. My father's done well
with his therapy dogs, their soft coats
bring back his days of raising hounds,
a young father, before the suits and ties,
before the suburbs. He loves best the room
which houses the war dogs exhibit,
old Rin Tin Tin and the Yorkie, Smoky.

As we enter the parking lot, circle
for a spot his chair can handle,
he starts to sing, he sings *Way Down Yonder
in the Land of Buttons*...he sings loudly,
his voice echoes across the lot, reaches
a woman walking her whippet, she's startled,
the dog turns toward us. My father
ignores the woman, says *isn't that the same dog
your friend had in high school? Wasn't she the friend
who died of a self-inflicted woe?
What happened to her dog? Was he sad, too?*
Before I can begin to answer,

my father starts to sing, he sings This Old Man—
knick knack paddywack, give the dog a bone!
This old man came rolling home. By the time
we travel the museum's ramp, he has sung
all ten verses, twice, and I'm Liza again, who mends.

PART THREE

I like crawfish, I like rice,
And I like girls that treat you nice—
—Guy Clark

When a female jury can't be counted on,
The end is near. Sweet sanity is gone.
—James Whitehead

The Origins of Geography

In 1966, my father bought a brand new
Pontiac Tempest with a cam engine,
the most beautiful thing I'd ever seen,
champagne colored, thick protective plastic
to preserve the luscious leather seats.
I was proud of that car, its sheer
American bulk and excess.
That was the year we drove to California,
my pink autograph book waiting for stars.
We drove all day, all night, my mother sharing
the wheel, candy and grilled cheese
at truck stops, the sheer joy of going far.
I remember the Grand Canyon, how I told
my sisters one day I'd live there, how I put
a good dent in my savings to buy costume
turquoise, a feather for my hair. In Las Vegas,
my father gambled while my mother walked
with us along Fremont Street, windows
full of glitter and sass. I bought her a black
cigarette holder, six inches of the truest
elegance I'd ever seen, loved watching
her long fingers twirl it as she puffed.

Then Disneyland and the promise of pleasure—
I loved most the talking Lincoln and the Tiki Room,
this beginning of a life of umbrella drinks
and the men who brought them, some as tall
and talkative as Mr. Lincoln himself,
but all of them eager to spend time, money
in places of mercy and darkness.
We'd saved so much for amusement, we dressed
to show it—girls in their summer dresses,
white leather shoes, bows and beads, beautiful

and worthy, our mother with her snap handbag
full of gum and crackers, our father's
pressed slacks. But one sister's shoes cut
into her feet, their crisscross ribbons dug
deeply enough to scar. The baby returned
from the restroom trailing toilet paper
under her ruffles, cried hard, harder
when we laughed, when a man said, *Hey there*
where you girls from? Who dresses up
for Disneyland? What's your origin?

I didn't know what that word suggested,
had not yet learned to think of birthplace
as stamp. Driving east again that very night,
I slept nearly to Winslow, woke in love
with the car again, my father's tanned arm
resting outside the window, the smell
of Wrigley's gum sweet and utterly
familiar. I had a story to tell everyone
in Joplin, gifts of ashtrays, shrunken heads,
a rabbit fur purse. I told everyone
I'd been out West. I told nobody
its geography of magic and shame.

When in St. Louis, Consider the Saint

But first you must indulge in the requisite
ride in the Arch, 631 feet of pentecostal
promise, sunstruck mandorla relecting
the urgent churn of the Mississippi below.
Stroll a ways to the Old Cathedral, light
a candle for your mother, your son, the dog
left to die on the tracks, all of the poor.
Eat toasted ravioli on The Hill, wander through
a church parking lot for fried chicken, or better,
pork steaks long cloaked in multiple bottles
of viscous sauce, served alongside baked onion,
sweet pickle and melon, ice-cold cans of Busch beer.
When in St. Louis, walk, eat, drink, and pray, but do
consider the saint himself, a mama's boy
at heart, no soldier that one. Consider
his long marriage to his teen sweetie,
their eleven alive children, his adored
possessions—the true Crown, a piece of the Cross.
And don't forget to consider his glorious
head of hair, powdery curls, masterful
layering, near-perfect texture. So when
in St. Louis enter a wig shop, try on
as many new selves as you can, try to believe
in each one, the mussed blonde, the sculpted redhead,
the coy brunette. Pay attention to the man
in the back booth, his tender touch as he adjusts
a woman's turban, tells her it'll all be OK, honey,
your new wig's got real attitude. Do all these
things while you can still speak, before the lump's
irreverent insistence, while you can still see
more than smoke and shadow, before the cane,
the chair, the bed, the gate. Witness and testify.

Ashes, Ashes, We'll All Fall Down

Old man Schmelzel (how we loved his name—
called him *Stinky Schmel* behind his back
until our father slapped us, said *you never*
insult a man who's given a leg
for his country, goddamn it, you don't),
sat on his back stoop and sullenly
tossed a rubber ball for his deaf dachshund,
a dog we liked to try to kiss through the chain link
until the old man caught us, told us
kissing dogs would give us dog teeth, our baby
teeth would fall out at night while we dreamed,
and in the morning we'd have fangs, would drool
and waddle, how we'd be a sincere
disappointment to our parents.
If he wasn't out back with his little dog,
Schmelzel was in a lawn chair out front,
his wooden leg pinocchioed before him,
the neighborhood ogre, that man,
for no reason but that he was.
He yelled at us for everything we were,
loud, dirty, quick in our bodies:
Where's the damn fire, he'd call,
slow down, you act like a bunch of barn cats,
slow down, no fire I see, you see smoke?
As long as our father wasn't outside
fussing with his tomato plants or drinking
beer, we'd hiss back, not loud enough
for anyone but us to hear—*We smell*
smoke, Old Stinky, there's fire everywhere.
We're on the run. We plan to burn alive.

Why I Like Some Country Songs

Johnny King's big sister Betsey taught baton
in the backyard of their house, the only
original farmhouse in the little
brick suburb where my sister and I grew
up. My sister studied the art of toss
and twirl, her shiny green streamers catching
sun, all sparkle, sparkle. My job was to walk
her home after class to supper and our
family's quiet nights of cards, coffee,
my mother's nick, nick, of knitting needles.
I loved the wait for her, how Betsey barked
out choreography, how all the girls
marched and panted. And I also loved
to watch Johnny King's daddy, the only man
for miles who wore overalls, worked on
engines not his own, not just to pass
a lazy Saturday. And Johnny King?
He was the boy I might have loved, all black
curls and a sideways smile. In fifth grade
he wrote an essay, first sentence—*The settlers
were captured by Narrative Americans—*
our teacher laughed, Johnny blushed, surprised,
sat inside the awkward claps of equally
confused classmates, but now I think I get it,
that Johnny might have known something fine
all along, must have had something of his sister's
grace and his father's skill, must have had a tale
or two worth telling, could capture a woman
and hold her. And if Johnny King had known
I could love him, I'd be the woman held,
the one who cleans the fish and washes the fruit,
boils the potatoes. I'd have a purpose
and a good heart, a man who came home most

every night with a story about how the wrist
can turn quite perfectly and make something fly,
how some things sputter to life with mere heat, some oil.

Saving Face

Nearly 35 years from today
she'll be asleep on a Sunday morning,
her second husband spooned against her,
the two cats cornered at the bottom
of the bed. She'll rise to the ring
of the telephone, shuffle through the hall
to the kitchen, leave the man, a carpenter
she's loved for years, loved from the day she knew
he could build her this house, its open spaces
and secrets (her name carved into a truss,
their own hand prints pushed into stucco),
she'll leave this man to sleep in. When she picks
up the telephone, it's her mother's voice,
coming to her from a little brick house
in the hometown she left decades ago,
and she'll hear that house in her mother's breath,
see its tidy lawn and tomato plants,
the rose trellis and the chain link fence,
the blind poodle, the fireflies, mosquitoes.
Her mother will say—*Oh, honey. It's bad
news. Laura Thompson has shot herself
through the heart, has saved her face, she's gone,
gone, she's done such a sad and common thing.*
This news will take its clear and careful time
to bring her down, but she will on that Sunday
morning go back to bed, back to the man
who loves her, his uncovered chest a mat
of black and grey, and she'll think of the wolf
come to blow a house down, and then she'll sleep
awhile, rise again, make coffee, break eggs.
But on this very day in 1969,
she and Laura Thompson ride a tandem
bike through neighborhoods they'll never live in.

Both she and Laura have boyfriends,
thirteen year olds with substantial Greek
names and the town's fullest promise. She and Laura
wear their heavy ID bracelets, talk of how
when they marry these boys they'll have porch lights
and horses, barns and patios, gardens
with statues, welcome mats at both screen doors.

And on this day Laura laughs from the front
seat of the bike, turns her soon to be
heartbreakingly beautiful face, says
Look! Look at that one! The people
in that house could be happy forever
as she pedals them farther and faster
through tall grass, toward deep woods, and into stone.

Story Problems

Every Sunday the same story, supper
of pot roast and potatoes, sweaty pitchers
of sweet tea, fruit pies or pudding or ice cream.
After she cleared the food away, our mother
worked at the kitchen sink in her lovely
apron, the one with cherry blossoms
and ruffles, her heavy rubber gloves
a squeak as she sponged the tile counters.

My sister and I would've gladly helped,
our own little aprons drawn snugly
around our waists, would loved to have worked
alongside her, so sure we were of becoming
her, of being beautiful and necessary.
But on Sundays after supper my father
helped with homework or taught us how to change
a tire or how to shimmy our bodies
out of basement windows during fire drills.

We dreaded Sundays after supper,
thought everything he meant to teach
unlovely, unnecessary: how many
girls did we see slithering out of windows?
Isn't there always someone to call
when a tire goes flat, some sweet boy?
And who cares if a train leaves one depot
at a certain time and another's coming
from the opposite direction at a certain speed,
who cares when they'll meet, when they'll
pass each other on some double tracks
in some never named small town? Who cares?

You got a cow on those tracks, you care,
our father said, and that became the mantra
my sister and I've shared for years: unplanned
pregnancies, failing grades or job searches,
failing marriages, bad investments, blood
tests, our country gone completely crazy,
so many cows on the tracks and no way
to save them, no skills to calculate
the coming trains. The moral here is pay
attention, listen up. Try this one:

If the California Zephyr, eastbound
at 38 miles per hour, goes through Verdi,
Nevada at 11:51 in the morning
and a Union Pacific freight, westbound
at 16 miles per hour, goes through Sparks,
Nevada at the same time, where will they pass?
The answer is that they'll pass right in front
of the house I now live in, where I'm cooking
pot roast and boiling potatoes this Sunday
afternoon, waiting for my lover to come,
there's a tire to be changed and a window's
broken, and I've got a story to tell
and I really need to tell it now.

I Miss Everyone in Amarillo

—sentiment on a card sent from a U.S Marine

This boy misses the smell of tortillas,
his mother's thick arms stretching
to serve, to clean, to refill, to care for.
A woman in Seattle misses her man,
his full-lipped face, the way he leans
against the sink, drinks milk.
A man outside St. Louis misses his wife,
how her face falls to one side as she sleeps,
how she carries the fragrance of soap, of bread.
A girl lying down to watch clouds pass above
somewhere in Nevada, believes she sees
her father, MIA for months, and closes her eyes.

This, then, must be the season of lost things:
lovers, children, the promise of hope,
all the dustings of love. This is the season
to miss, to lose. You know, I'm not always
a sentimental girl, but goddamn it.

Aunt Mabel and the Legless Veteran

Robert knows he's lucky to be an assistant
professor in a small college town in a southern
state where everyone loves his school,
has a regional tolerance for many
oddities associated with academics,
but his arrest for drunken driving
still stings, picture in the paper, a bad
one, the suspended license rendering
him back to biking the town like a grad
student, and now he's to choose
his community service: 20 hours folding clothes
at Goodwill or a weekend with Herb,
a nearly blind senior citizen
known to tire most caretakers within minutes
with long walks and longer stories.
Robert chooses Herb, tells his young and very
pregnant wife, how bad could it be?

On Saturday, there are many stops
for groceries, prescriptions, cigarettes.
Herb buys one pack of Camels each month,
says even the ridiculous sin tax
can't stop him, he's like anyone's old
Aunt Mabel, he lives alone and needs some
pleasure, and if that comes to him by striking
a match and taking a long drag, those bastards
have no compassion, who do they think fought
the commies, and how do they think men became
friends? Sharing smokes, that's how. So the voters
are actually against friendship, see, and against
allowing a lonely old woman some
pleasure as she leans out her window, sits
on her own porch. Herb says his baby daughter

was a smoker, and imagining Herb
as a young father, Robert thinks this woman
must be in her fifties now, full of flesh,
how hard it must be to see your own daughter
as middle aged, how hard to know she's probably
desired by no man, and then Herb says she's dead,
her brain exploded, when they cut her open
and divvied up her parts, her lungs were good,
went, Herb's sure, to a lesser human.

On Sunday there are no necessary
errands, so Herb wants to walk all day,
mosey down to the railroad tracks, watch
for a BNSF engine, not common,
but most certainly beautiful, Herb and his
wife rode the Super Chief on their honeymoon,
went west to see Indians, he bought her
a blossom necklace, they ate on real china
in the dining car, there were most certainly
movie stars on board, his wife wore white gloves.
His daughter, Herb says, once rode the Amtrak
from Seattle to Chicago just to meet
him for a Cubs game, she was that good a girl.
Outside the stadium sat a legless
man with a sign—Vet Needs Help—and they gave
him ten dollars, it was so obvious
the man wasn't faking it, had really
no legs, so, Herb says, a fin each seemed OK,
but you can't trust everyone with a sign,
some of them are just lazy, some fools,
some bona fide drug addicts. But a legless
old man, vet or not, sure could use a cold one
and a dog, right? Right, Mr. Smarty Pants?

On his way home to his lovely wife,
Robert stops to buy her a carton
of lemonade, her craving today.
He leans his bike against the newspaper stand,
imagines who will walk next with Herb,
how riding a bike around town isn't
really all that bad, but maybe if he took
up walking he'd have more time to think
and maybe he'd think of a name for his
unborn daughter and maybe it will be
an old-fashioned name like Edna or Thelma
or Ethel or Miriam or Mabel.
That's it. Maybelle. That's what he'll tell his wife
tonight as she drinks lemonade, he gin.

Oklahoma was OK

She thinks often of the long year they lived
in Tulsa, how she loved that city,
its aggressive winter and sticky
summer spent on porches, sweet tea, baseball
on the radio, all crackle and crackle
and the sparkle of fireflies. She loved
Jamil's, the infrequent treat of steak,
appetizer of fried bologna
and olives, loved the Mexican place
on 15th Street, first taste of cilantro
exotic as perfume, her own perfume
a running joke with the black bus driver:
I just love your White Shoulders, missy.
She loved the old Camelot Hotel,
beautiful and absurd as the Prayer Tower,
the liquor-by-the-wink laws that kept
her purse full of club cards and promise,
loved the old brick apartment house they shared
with day laborers and secretaries,
how thin the walls were, how tired and angry
their neighbors, the screaming all night,
how so unlike those people she and he were,
how much they laughed then. He called out to her
Stella, I'm home and she called, *Oh, Stanley,*
every day a new act. The show went on,
they were easy in their bodies then,
and in their hearts and talk. All was OK
before some coming rage, before they learned
that games of house and family
are often played with sticks, easily burned.

If he reads this, he should call her. Just think:
they'd be strangers again, capable of kindness.

Come, Sit, Touch, Stay, Settle

Every Saturday on the way to the dog's
obedience class where she is learning
basic commands that will allow her to live
in my house, fit in, be a companion,
I pass the apartment building along the river
where you lived those months before we finalized.
Today two children sat near the goldfish pond,
and I remembered our sitting there,
breaking the ice with aspen branches
in an early October winter,
our effort to free the fish one thing
we both fought for. I never told you
about the time when you still lived in the house,
how I drove back to that house, how I sat
in my car and watched you through the window,
watched you wander from room to room, touch
the books in their cases, sit, settle down
into a chair, rise again for another
book, touch, touch, touch. I imagined you
trying to find the right story, trying
to understand how some other could've called
my name, could've left you alone to stay.
But there was no calling, no burlap bag
over the head, no choker, pinch or shock,
no lure. There was a soft spot in the soil,
soft enough to dig under the fence,
find the path to the river, its rushing
away, the smell of fish and brush
and marvelous decay, so very much.

Maybe we should have had a dog. Maybe
we'd have had one that always came when called.

Provisions for a Long Marriage

Her husband watches the weather channel
is always one she can count on to say
how humid the day will be in far away
Cincinnati, or Jersey, Shreveport
or Seattle, facts he shares as evidence
he loves her. This she is sure of.

So when he says *a big storm's coming in,*
need to run to town, stock up for several
days, these Sierra roads will be impassable,
impossible to get out safely,
she trusts him. He says, *what do we need?*
What do you really want? What's essential?

She hears him, hears too Billie Holiday
on the radio, voice a fragile grit
of hope, of vacuum, of what's lost and what
little's left come every winter.
She remembers a story: how Billie
gave her lover a grocery list, daily
essentials: cigarettes, gin, dog food.

Like Billie, she wants the gin, a sturdy
pack of Marlboros, really needs the dog food.
No one in her house should hunger or be cold.
But there's more that's needed, so bring, she says,
red lipstick, the one made by Revlon,
and a nail polish to match, no, better,
bring me the long press-on nails, sharp enough

to tear fabric or the small silly spot
on your back, bring me black nylons,
the thigh-high kind, let's make this easy,

oh, and bring those eyelashes in a little
plastic box, make sure they're extra long
and thick, I want to make you sneeze
when I lick your neck. And a dress?
Red or black, you choose, but make certain
you like it, that the thin straps are those most
willing to slip down with the breeze of a wink.

But what she really says as they both
prepare for the snows ahead is *bring milk,*
bring salt, bring flour and wine, some sugar
and cinnamon, a really soft cheese.
I'll build a fire, run a bath, bake something
sweet. Drive carefully, my dear. Come home safe.

Tomato, Saint, Song

—for Leonard Sanazaro

A woman whose garden I ardently
admire, covet, envious of the way
whatever she touches blooms, will thrive,
will bring forth fruit no one could buy, blessed
her hands must be, this woman, let's call her
Veronica, reminds me each spring
not to over-water my tomato plants,
to remember (*don't forget!*) that tomatoes,
to come full and ripe by July, must suffer,
must think that making fruit is urgent,
must sag a bit, crust the edge of their leaves.
But every summer I water and water,
I love the big, lush green of their being
alive, think I can wait for their certain
reward, one I'll hold in my hand to eat.

When in her voice I hear its admonition,
I think of how it's been years since you roped
your neck to a garage truss, your dog well fed
and asleep upstairs. I've stopped thinking
that if I'd been there in time, I could've touched
your face, taken the sweat, the heat,
away with a soft cloth, one that would always
have something of you in it, eternal.
But I did find the new poems hidden
in your nightstand, your work full of blood
and promise, green work, but lush in image,
your sense of agency and urgency in each lie.

So, gone friend, this is my promise
not to forget, to think of you sometimes
like I do today as I stand here

at the open kitchen window, the early
autumn air crisp and crepuscular.
I have a ripe tomato in my hand,
there's a Guy Clark song on the radio,
a really good one. It's a Friday. I'm here.

On Turning Fifty

Annie says the small joys of my new AARP card
will dissipate quickly, my delight in its discounts
a peasant rush of fun so fleeting I'll not remember
it in a mere few years. We're having lunch
on the patio of a little bistro near campus,
Cobb salads and raspberry tea, I'm buying,
my card's on the table. Students move briskly
around us, all heat and bone and the flush of blood.
Annie, who's sixty, says the hourglass figure
she was famous for became a Dali rendering,
its sands settled so deep there was no hope
that Dorothy could be saved. And her hair,
she says, look how fine now, except on
my face, I pluck my chin every morning,
and what bitter god thought that up?
And then there's the question of screwing—
hormones or not? Crap the heart and save
the juice or live long to pluck, pluck, pluck?
And those heels? Think you'll be wearing those
come December? Think you'll be able to wear
a sweater? I'm playing with the egg on my plate,
my sense of triumph (a half century!) in complete
shadow, when around the corner comes
one of the world's most virile, most beautiful
things—a newly waxed, slow-moving fire truck,
house bound. Two firemen ride the runners,
our side of the street, and as they pass,
they smile, sweet smiles, they wave. Annie touches
her fingers to her throat, looks up into the sun.
I drink long from my cold glass, cross, recross
my legs. When the truck's out of sight, Annie says
oh, hell—let's get a bottle of wine. Let's drink it all.

Ain't Nothing

Ain't nothing sexier than a snaggletoothed
woman, my uncles used to tell me,
their bottles of beer or glasses, bourbon
and branch, balanced elegantly near
their knees or on the arms of Kennedy rockers
that graced my grandmother's front porch, full
bellies, all of us, chicken and biscuits, cobbler.

I believed them about the woman
because I knew they loved me and because
I had to, my own smile a slash of well-worn
gravel, my destiny quite often noted
by cousins—*that girl's gonna need some real work.*

Once, years later, way after some work
had been done but before the long years
of losses, I asked another man,
one I loved, about the sexy woman,
had he heard that before, was it true?
He hadn't. It wasn't. And that was that.

About the Author

Gailmarie Pahmeier has lived most of her life in Nevada. She teaches creative writing and contemporary literature courses at the University of Nevada, Reno where she has been honored with the Alan Bible Teaching Excellence Award and the University Distinguished Teacher Award. She is also on the faculty of the low residency MFA Program at Sierra Nevada College.

A frequent Pushcart Prize nominee, her work has garnered a number of awards, including a Witter Bynner Poetry Fellowship and two Artists Fellowships from the Nevada Arts Council and has been widely published in literary journals and anthologies. She is the author of *The House on Breakaheart Road* and three chapbooks, the most recent of which, *Shake It and It Snows*, won the 2009 Coal Hill Chapbook Award from Autumn House Press. In 2007, she received the Governor's Award for Excellence in the Arts from the state of Nevada. She serves as Poet-in-Residence for her state and was a National Literary Panelist for the YoungArts program.

Colophon

Designed and produced by Robert Blesse at the Black Rock
Press, Department of Art, School of the Arts, University of
Nevada, Reno. The typeface is Chapparal Pro, designed by
Carol Twombly for Adobe Systems. Printed and bound by
BookMobile in Minneapolis